WAR GAMES

ANDREW BURTCH · MARIE-LOUISE DERUAZ

CANADIAN WAR MUSEUM
MUSÉE CANADIEN DE LA GUERRE

Library and Archives Canada Cataloguing in Publication

Title: War games / Andrew Burtch and Marie-Louise Deruaz.

Names: Burtch, Andrew Paul, 1978- author. | Deruaz, Marie-Louise, author. | Canadian War Museum, issuing body.

Series: Souvenir catalogue series ; 31.

Description: Series statement: Souvenir catalogue series ; 31 | Issued also in French under title: Jeux de guerre.

Identifiers: Canadiana 20230188087 | ISBN 9780660457161 (softcover)

Subjects: LCSH: War games—History— Exhibitions. | LCSH: Military miniatures— Exhibitions. | LCSH: War—Computer simulation—Exhibitions. | LCSH: Video games in art—Exhibitions. | LCSH: War in art— Exhibitions. | LCGFT: Exhibition catalogs.

Classification: LCC U310 .B87 2023 | DDC 793.9/2074—dc23

Published by the
Canadian War Museum
1 Vimy Place
Ottawa, ON K1A 0M8
warmuseum.ca

Printed and bound in Canada.

Graphic design by: nineSixteen Creative.

TABLE OF CONTENTS

FOREWORD

Organized conflict, sadly, is perhaps humankind's most terrible creation. Violent, destructive and ferociously complex, it has horrified and fascinated in near-equal measure.

I welcome the launch of the **War Games** exhibition and its accompanying catalogue. Together, they contribute to public understanding of the intimate relationship between war and society.

War informed our imaginations and nightmares long before it entered our military academies as grim practice, or our gaming consoles as frenetic leisure. The boundaries between play and preparation were, and remain, permeable. Young medieval lords played with toy knights before maturing to more earnest practice in arms. Idle social games of strategy taught decision making and the vicissitudes of chance. Professionals at arms learned to plan operations on huge maps or sand tables — the deadly serious precursors to fun games with wooden blocks, counters, or miniature figures.

Popular attitudes always infused representations of conflict. In 19th and early 20th century Europe, small, brightly painted soldiers communicated national pride, but not national responsibility for the barbarity of colonial conquests or the ravages of modern weaponry. The reverse was also true, with conflict and games informing public attitudes, homogenizing complex issues, or objectifying presumed enemies.

Government propaganda and commercial marketing entwined, producing games and merchandise that also served as platforms for messages and sales — pitches that were in turn shaped by contemporary events, diplomacy, literature and espionage.

East-West tensions in the 1980s sparked a minor publishing bonanza, feeding a small industry of hypothetical war games that subsequently became vehicles for the training of military recruits.

Each type of war game has its own sub-genre, from tactical instruction to computer simulation, from strategic planning to hobby collecting. All are closely related.

War Games reflects what we have thought about war throughout history, shaping it through our creativity, fears and hopes, and being shaped by it as well. It is about entertainment and education, pop culture, and professional excellence. Thank you for considering these themes with us.

Dean F. Oliver
Interim Vice-President and Director General
Canadian War Museum

INTRODUCTION

War, play and games have long and interconnected histories. War is not a game, but militaries have used war games to innovate, adapt and train, and wars have shaped the games people play.

From the games and toys of the world wars, to wargaming contemporary global crises, both hobby games and professional military games reflect the concerns of their time.

This exhibition tells the story of wargaming. It reveals how military personnel have developed and adapted games to meet challenges, and explores how civilians have learned about war through play.

War Games offers a sampling of the vast range of activities encompassed by war games throughout history and across cultures.

From ancient dice-rolling games and tabletop wars fought with lead soldiers, to the computer-simulated environments and enemies that characterize arena-packing e-sports, bloodless contests of will and wit between gamers have long been used as forms of training and experimentation to potentially gain an advantage in contemporary or future conflicts.

Some of the players featured in this exhibition, like British novelist H. G. Wells, hoped that their mock wars might replace the actual bloody affair. Others have used games as a medium to critique war and convey its terrible impacts to diverse audiences.

While some view games as entertainment from which little can be learned or gained, the **War Games** exhibition offers a chance to examine games that have had an important historical impact, and how wars have clearly shaped the games we play.

CHAPTER 1

WAR AND GAMES: FROM ANTIQUITY TO THE PRESENT

Games about war and battle have existed across different cultures for thousands of years.

Some were games of chance, while others were strategy games or games that helped teach players tactics for battle. Games also served to settle differences through play, instead of turning to actual bloodshed.

Many of these games are still played today and may have influenced the games you play.

Artwork showing the introduction of chess to the Persian court, 6th century CE

Pawn from a Ukrainian-style chess set

A War Game

This 2,500-year-old decorated amphora (ceramic vessel) features two Greek heroes of the Trojan War — Achilles and Ajax — leaning on their spears as they play a game. They may be playing *Petteia*, a game of skill in which players attempted to entrap their opponent's pieces.

Black-figure amphora showing Achilles and Ajax playing a game, c. 525 BCE >

<> Crystal die from Rome,
c. 300 BCE (left), stone
die from Egypt (right)

A Roll of the Dice

Games that simulate war often include an element of chance
to determine the outcomes of mock battles with game pieces.

Dice have long been used to introduce chance into games.
These six-sided dice date back to Roman and Egyptian
games played approximately 2,300 years ago.

Strategic Thinking

Go, an ancient strategy game that is still popular today, originated in China approximately 2,500 years ago.

Taking turns placing their white or black stones on a grid, players attempt to encircle or capture their opponent's stones and control the most territory on the board. Much as commanders would do on the battlefield, one game strategy involves dividing the opponent's forces into ineffective groups and forcing their retreat.

Canadian Go Association event in Vancouver, British Columbia, July 1, 2017 >

A Game of Kings

Chess originated in India as *Chaturanga*, a game with pieces that represented the forces in a battle — soldiers, chariots, war elephants, and cavalry. The game changed as it spread to Persia, and from there to the Middle East, Europe, and Asia. As the rules and game pieces evolved, one constant remained: victory hinged on the fate of one piece — the king.

< **Chess piece (knight)**
from Iraq, 9th century

The Elder Brothers Chess Set

Kanien'kehá:ka (Mohawk) artist Angel Doxtater, from Six Nations of the Grand River, made this chess set with traditional corn-husk doll game pieces. The pieces represent the "elder brothers" of the Hodinohso:ni Confederacy — the Kanien'kehá:ka — made with purple flint-corn husks, and the Onödowá'ga (Seneca), made with white corn husks.

This set reflects Hodinohso:ni history and culture. The pawns hold water drums, the rooks lacrosse sticks, and the kings Two Row Wampum Belts, representing the 1613 treaty between the Hodinohso:ni and early Dutch settlers in what is now New York. The two rows of purple beads signify peace, mutual respect, and non-interference in each other's affairs.

**The Elder Brothers by
Angel Doxtater, 2020** >

ANGEL DOXTATER

Kanien'kehá:ka (Mohawk) artist

PERSPECTIVE

Angel explains why she created
The Elder Brothers chess set:

> "We're an oppressed people,
> we're the product of an attempted
> genocide and assimilation. And part
> of [*The Elder Brothers*] chess set is
> to show that fight. We're still here.
> You know, we're still here, and our
> traditional councils are still in place."

CHAPTER 2

THE WORLD WARS

The First World War (1914–1918) and Second World War (1939–1945) were fought around the world and were preceded by extensive planning. Training and analytical games helped militaries study the challenges of anticipated battles and prepare strategies.

War held sway over those who served and those who supported them from the home front. During the wars, toys, games and popular pastimes reflected and were influenced by wartime events.

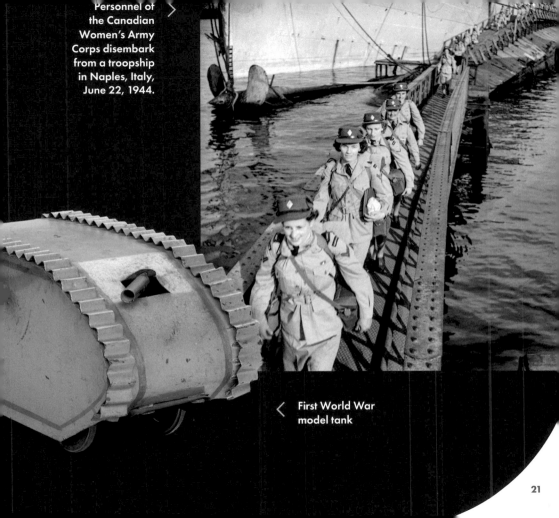

Personnel of the Canadian Women's Army Corps disembark from a troopship in Naples, Italy, June 22, 1944.

First World War model tank

THE ROAD TO THE FIRST WORLD WAR

Professional military war games became widespread across Europe and North America following the Prussians' stunning victory in the Franco-Prussian War (1870–1871). Soon after, militaries adopted Prussian (German) training tools, including the *Kriegspiel* (war game), which had been used since the mid-1800s.

In the years leading up to the First World War, armies used war games to train officers in strategic thinking and to prepare for war.

Illustration showing the
headquarters staff of
25th Battalion (County of
London) Cyclist Regiment
playing a war game similar
to *The Game of War*, 1909

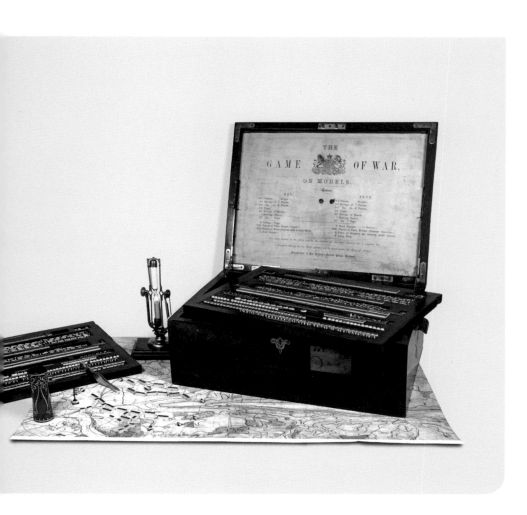

The Game of War

British Army officers used *The Game of War* in the 1880s to simulate detailed operations on accurate maps. More than 1,500 game pieces represented infantry, cavalry and signals, as well as obstacles. Each turn, players had limited time to draft orders for units to move, attack or fortify positions on the map. A roll of the dice determined whether or not an attack was successful.

Canada ordered similar war game sets from the British War Office in the years prior to the First World War.

In *The Game of War*, each game box contained hundreds of pieces, allowing players to simulate small unit battles, as well as complicated clashes between army divisions or corps.

Little Wars

British author H. G. Wells, who is best known for writing science fiction novels such as *The War of the Worlds*, was also an enthusiastic miniature gamer.

In 1913, he published *Little Wars*, which detailed rules for a war game using tin soldiers. At the end of his rule book, he declared his hope that such games could replace the need for actual wars, avoiding all the harm and bloodshed they bring.

Toy soldiers from H. G. Wells's personal collection were used in mock battles before the First World War and long afterwards by his son and grandchildren.

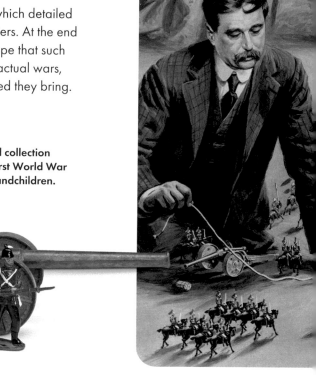

Depiction of H. G. Wells (left) playing *Little Wars,* 1913

Stahl und Eisen (Coal and Steel)

Players of this 1915 German game started
at the gates of a wartime factory to learn
how steel was transformed into weapons
and how coal fuelled the German Navy.

This game board follows coal from
the mines to the front lines.

HMCS Ville de Québec
Gets a Sub by Commander
Harold Beament, 1943

REFINING TACTICS IN THE SECOND WORLD WAR

For Canada and the Allies, the Second World War's naval operations were crucial to victory, as vast quantities of war supplies crossed the Atlantic Ocean to support fighting fronts in Europe and Russia. The enemy — German U-boats — threatened the lifeline, and Allied victory with it.

War games could not predict the outcome of the war at sea, but they were an important tool in preparing warship and convoy commanders to face the enemy threat.

The Western Approaches Tactical Unit

By 1942, German submarines were sinking hundreds of thousands of tonnes of Allied shipping each month.

In January 1942, Captain Gilbert Roberts of the Royal Navy was tasked with setting up the Western Approaches Tactical Unit (WATU) in Liverpool, England. The WATU team used war games to test new approaches, tactics and weapons that convoys could use to locate and destroy U-boats.

Composed primarily of members of the Women's Royal Naval Service (WRNS, often called Wrens), the team first played through scenarios to understand how the U-boats attacked, and then used games to train naval officers in new tactics to counter submarine attacks against Allied convoys.

Wrens plot convoy and U-boat positions on the floor at the WATU, 1945.

Officers attending a WATU course peer through a screen to plot their next move in a mock convoy battle, March 18, 1945.

WATU Souvenir

Naval officer Helen Coop, originally from Liverpool, served in the Western Approaches Tactical Unit (WATU) during the war. She plotted students' moves during mock submarine battles using game pieces like this one.

Game piece representing an escort ship in the tactical games played at the WATU

THE WAR IN YOUR LIVING ROOM

Games and toys that found their way into homes reflected both the urgency of conflict and the challenges faced by the soldiers, sailors and pilots who were fighting battles on land, at sea, and in the air.

Fighting with the Allies, a world-war-themed, Canadian-made board game, was released as Canadian soldiers entered the war in 1915.

Fighting
WITH THE ALLIES

The NEW
WAR GAME

Originated, Designed &
MADE IN CANADA

Copyright 1915. by F.V. Banks.

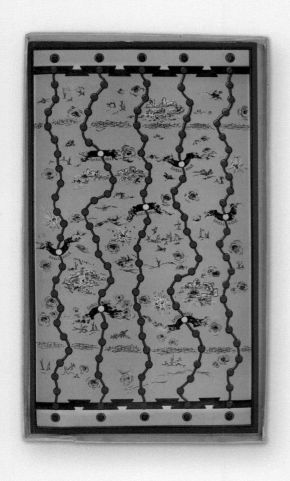

The American game *Over There* was published in 1918, after the United States entered the war.

38

Wir Fahren Gegen Engeland (Driving Against England)

Players of this 1940 German game took on the roles of German submarine commanders patrolling the British Isles to sink Royal Navy warships. The player who sank the most shipping tonnage won the game.

Whenever a real British ship was sunk by a German U-boat, the original owner of this game noted the details on the back of the playing cards.

On the back of the game card for HMS *Royal Oak*, the game's original owner noted "Sunk by Lieutenant-Commander [Gunther] Prien in the bay of Scapa Flow October 14, 1939."

A Reminder from Overseas

In 1940, Captain Joseph Samuel Corbett fashioned this toy Spitfire fighter plane from the wreckage of a German Dornier bomber that was shot down near his camp in the United Kingdom.

A friend brought this Spitfire model home to Toronto to Corbett's wife, Clarice, and his two-year-old son, Hugh, during the Second World War.

CHAPTER 3

THE COLD WAR: GAMING THE UNIMAGINABLE

During the Cold War (1946–1991), the tension between the United States and the Soviet Union could have led to a devastating nuclear war.

As opponents, these countries armed themselves with growing stockpiles of nuclear weapons, and joined military alliances to deter each other from attack.

Nuclear war — if it occurred — would have unthinkable consequences, killing billions of people. But in war games, future conflict scenarios could be simulated safely. Fear of a deadly third world war was also echoed in the games that were played during the Cold War.

Lieutenant-Colonel W. Arthur Croteau points to ground zero of an atomic explosion over Ottawa during a war game, 1952.

This "Nike" toy rocket, made for children, shared a name with a U.S. Army nuclear-tipped, surface-to-air missile.

43

A SERIOUS HOBBY

As the Cold War rivalry between the superpowers intensified and the prospect of a war became frighteningly real, a new game industry emerged to simulate past, current and future conflicts.

Toy soldiers were increasingly replaced by cheaper and more complicated hobby games in which war could be fought on maps with game pieces. The war game industry was inspired by military developments, and, in turn, militaries used or adapted commercial war games to help train future leaders.

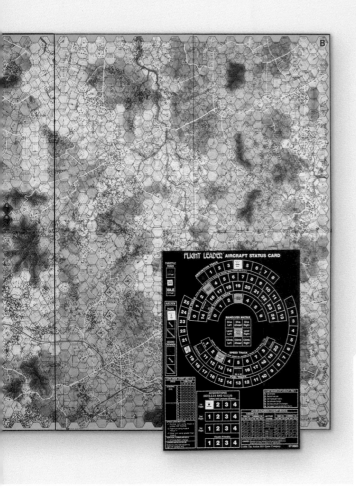

Several popular Avalon Hill games, such as *Flight Leader*, were first developed under contract to the American military and later released commercially.

War Games in the Soviet Union

The scenarios of hobby games in the Soviet Union reflected Soviet military strategy against Western democracies during the Cold War.

Vozdushny Boi (Dogfight) simulated an air battle over Europe, with the aim of destroying the other player's planes and airfields.

***Vozdushny Boi*
game box and board**

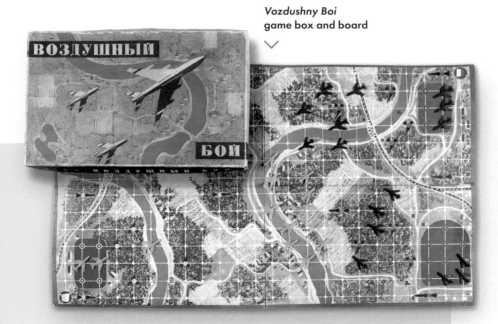

Canadian Wargamer

Before the advent of the Internet, it was difficult to find other experienced and enthusiastic hobby war game players. Gamers turned to magazines and other periodicals to locate players and game reviews, and to share ideas for new games. This self-published magazine, *Canadian Wargamer*, ran from 1967 to the 1970s.

Canadian
Wargamer,
Summer 1970

The Role-Playing Game

The world's most popular role-playing game, *Dungeons and Dragons*, began in the 1970s as the war game *Chainmail*, which simulated medieval warfare. Inspired by J. R. R. Tolkien's *The Lord of the Rings*, the designers later introduced fantasy elements. Players role play as wizards, fighters and clerics who adventure together, fighting creatures and completing quests.

Role-playing games paved the way for more complex storytelling and scenarios in games that came later.

A tabletop battle fought with miniatures unfolds in a game of *Dungeons and Dragons*.

Colourful box of the first edition of *Dungeons and Dragons*

DANIEL KWAN

Game designer, consultant and creator of the award-winning *Asians Represent!* podcast

PERSPECTIVE

Daniel describes role-playing games
and the impact of *Dungeons and Dragons*:

"What started as a niche hobby
game in the early 1970s has grown
into a global phenomenon. Because
Dungeons and Dragons has gone
global, we see different perspectives,
we see different people playing
these games and making their
own games. We see this exchange
in world-building ideas, cultural
experiences, and game designs."

Preparing for Future War

By the 1950s, Central Europe was the most militarized place on earth. The North Atlantic Treaty Organization (NATO) and the Soviet-aligned Warsaw Pact countries amassed conventional and nuclear weapons in anticipation of a third world war.

To prepare for future wars, NATO engaged in extensive field exercises involving tens of thousands of troops. Military officers also simulated future wars through tabletop war games to envision what would happen if the Cold War went hot.

Tanks cross a ribbon bridge spanning the Meuse River, in the Netherlands, during an American military training exercise, Operation Autumn Forge/Reforger 83.

The *Dunn-Kempf* War Game

In 1975, interest in wargaming as a training tool was surging. Captains Hilton Dunn and Steven Kempf, at the U.S. Army's Command and General Staff College, used scale-model tanks and helicopters to simulate a "Red" Soviet attack against "Blue" American forces in Germany. Similar games were adopted and used in training by the Canadian Army.

The Blue and Red teams used six-sided dice and calculators to see if their attacks succeeded. The game's objective was to teach tactical lessons to the players.

‹ U.S. Army officers play through a battle on the *Dunn-Kempf* set at Fort Leavenworth, Kansas, 1980s.

INTO THE COMPUTER AGE: FEAR AND FASCINATION

Militaries were the first, and largest, users of early computer technology. Computers helped in the development of nuclear weapons and communications networks, as well as with the monitoring of air defence. Computerized games allowed users to conduct and visualize complex war simulations.

The military investment in computers led to smaller, faster machines that could be marketed to consumers. Video games, which were initially side projects in computer laboratories, grew into a lucrative industry.

In 1958, the Navy Electronic Warfare Simulator was installed at the United States Naval War College. The system took up two floors of a building and was used to visualize mock naval battles.

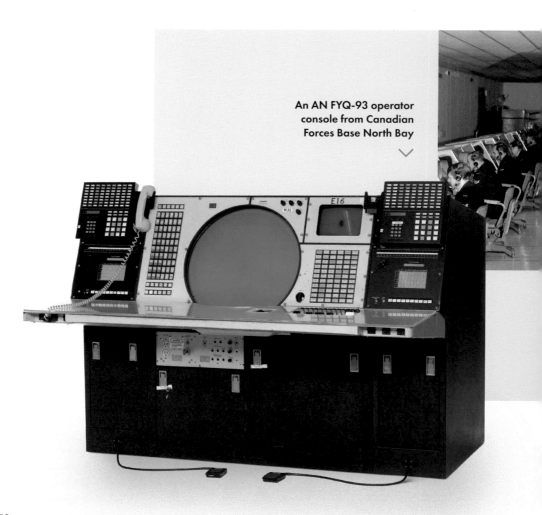

An AN FYQ-93 operator console from Canadian Forces Base North Bay

Watching and Waiting

Computer consoles like the AN FYQ-93 could display early signs of an attack, as operators monitored Canadian airspace for hostile or unidentified aircraft.

From 1963 to 2006, information from radar warning systems filtered into the consoles at the Canadian Forces Base North Bay Underground Complex — a four-storey operations centre tunnelled into the Canadian Shield and designed to withstand a nuclear attack. Operators using the consoles could help direct interceptor aircraft to investigate unauthorized flights or Soviet probes into North American airspace.

The Blue Room at the Canadian Forces Base North Bay Underground Complex, 1972

The Arcade Phenomenon

It did not take long for computer technology to find entertainment applications. The first video games were developed in military and civilian research laboratories, but they soon became fixtures in video arcades that evolved into a global subculture by the 1970s.

Crowded, dimly lit parlours in shopping malls and on city blocks blared the sounds of electronic war. Popular games drew crowds of young people ready to insert quarters into the newest games to try to beat other players' high scores.

Playing *Space Invaders* in a Santa Cruz arcade, 1981

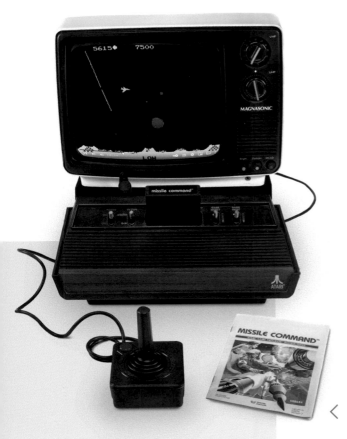

Gaming the War at Home

Home gaming experienced a boom in the 1970s and early 1980s, driven by the popular Atari television gaming console. The Atari games *Missile Command* and *Battlezone* appeared in arcades in 1979 and 1980, and were later released for the Atari home system.

< In *Missile Command*, players launched missiles to protect cities from nuclear destruction. It was impossible to win the game, much like nuclear war.

CHAPTER 4

GAMES AND THE WAR ON TERRORISM: 2001–2014

The end of the Cold War gave way to a series of conflicts that threatened world security.

An unexpected threat emerged when terrorists attacked the United States on September 11, 2001. The military response to those attacks, and the increased public security measures in many countries, became known as the "war on terror."

The largest conflicts in that war were in Afghanistan, whose government sheltered the terrorists who had launched the attacks, and in Iraq, which was invaded by a United States-led coalition in 2003.

Popular culture — including video games — reflected, questioned and promoted these wars, while contemporary war games explored conflicts of that time and the moral questions that accompanied them.

THE OFFICIAL U.S. ARMY GAME

AMERICA'S A★A ARMY

INCLUDES FULL VERSION OF
AMERICA'S ARMY GAME

SPECIAL FORCES
ENGINEER SGT.

18 CHARLIE

THE SPECIAL FORCES
ENGINEER SERGEANT
IS THE DEMOLITIONS
EXPERT. HE CAN
BUILD OR DESTROY
VIRTUALLY ANY TYPE
OF STRUCTURE. DUTIES
INCLUDE DEMOLITIONS,
CONSTRUCTION OF
FIELD FORTIFICATIONS,
TOPOGRAPHIC SURVEYS,
BRIDGING, RIGGING,
RECONNAISSANCE
AND A WIDE VARIETY OF
CIVIL ACTION PROJECTS.

FIGURE + GAME

SPECIAL FORCES.

TEEN
T
ESRB

RadioActiveClown

WARNING: CHOKING HAZARD
Small Parts. Not for children under 3 Years.

∧
A Canadian surveillance
drone launches in Kabul,
Afghanistan, 2003.

<
Promotional action
figure for the *America's
Army* video game.

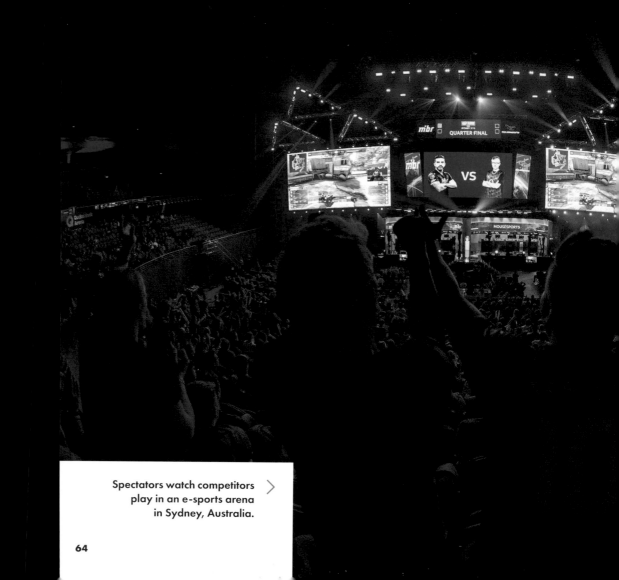

Spectators watch competitors
play in an e-sports arena
in Sydney, Australia. 〉

FROM THE ARCADE TO THE BLOCKBUSTER

By the early 2000s, global video game sales showed that the pastime had become enormously popular. Gamers left behind the arcade to stay home and play games on computers, mobile devices, and video game consoles such as PlayStation and Xbox.

War-themed games based on historical or contemporary conflicts sold millions of copies and, as with other fighting and strategy games, became popular avenues for competitive play.

War in the First Person

Most early video games simulated conflict from a birds-eye view. Beginning in the 1990s, a new type of video game transported players into the boots of soldiers and commandos on the ground.

As so-called "first-person shooter" games grew in popularity, parents and critics raised concerns that graphic depictions of violence and consequence-free simulations of gunplay would diminish players' understanding of violence.

In the first-person shooter game *Wolfenstein 3D*, players fight through a Second World War German compound from an American soldier's perspective.

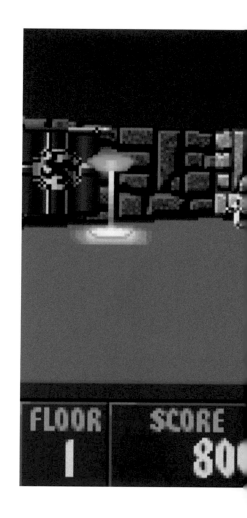

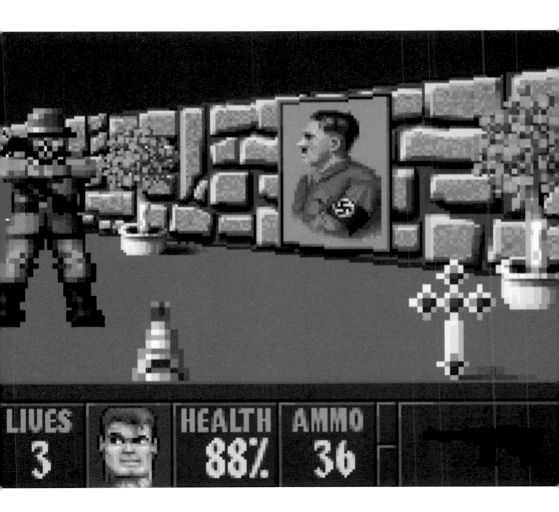

LIVES 3   HEALTH 88%   AMMO 36

Modern Warfare

Before the outbreak of the wars in Afghanistan and Iraq, in 2001 and 2003, most popular video games explored key battles in the Second World War.

By 2007, new war game franchises reflected the increasingly urgent threats of terrorism and counter-insurgency. The games, like the wars they emulated, led to controversy and debate over how wars — both real and virtual — were fought.

Medal of Honor, a first-person shooter game released in 2010, was set in the context of the Afghanistan War. In the original multiplayer mode, gamers could choose to play as the Taliban.

DR. RICHARD LACHMAN

**RTA School of Media,
Toronto Metropolitan University**

PERSPECTIVE

Richard explains that while gaming has some beneficial aspects, concerns linger about gaming and behaviours:

> "Games, like movies, perpetuate stereotypes of what villains might be, what a hero looks like . . . The nature of some of our online interactions can cause lasting harm — to women, to people of colour, or other groups that are bullied and targeted and threatened. This is a problem we have to address."

September 12th: A Toy World, developed by former journalist Gonzola Frasca and the Uruguayan game studio Newsgaming, critiqued the West's military responses to terrorist threats.

CRITICAL GAMES

Not all video games present war as entertainment. Some of the games that emerged during the Afghanistan and Iraq wars asked hard questions about the way modern wars are waged.

Certain game designers use the video game medium to ask players how they might react in times of war. While some games put the players in a position of power, critical games render the players powerless instead, at the mercy of war. Others, still, expose how conflicts can perpetuate a cycle of violence and extremism.

Surviving the War

You only have enough medicine to treat half of your family. Who should get it?

This War of Mine, developed by Polish company 11 bit studios, was inspired by the siege of Sarajevo, Bosnia-Herzegovina (1992–1995), in which approximately 5,000 civilians were killed.

In most war games, civilians are absent. In this game, players play only as civilians, caught in a war zone as they try to survive amid the ruins of their city.

< Screen capture from *This War of Mine* showing the ruined house in which players must try to survive the war

Killbox

In 2015, artist Joseph DeLappe, together with artists and game developers from Biome Collective, created an interactive art installation intended to critically explore drone warfare.

The installation allows users to experience the same fictionalized event from two perspectives: that of a drone pilot zeroing in on and attacking a target, and the attack experienced by a villager on the ground. The installation was inspired by American drone strikes documented in northern Pakistan between 2004 and 2015.

Two *Killbox* players interact with the installation at EGX London, 2015. They are participating in the same experience, but each in a different role.

[K I L L B O X]
A GAME ABOUT DRONE WARFARE

www.killbox.info

@ inthekillbox

inthekillbox

RECRUITING

The popularity of military-themed, first-person shooter games led to new avenues for military recruitment. If nothing else, games offered a means to inform the public about military equipment, ethics and career opportunities.

In this era, military and civilian gaming became more closely intertwined. However, this development was controversial because of the association of military service with a pastime popular with children and youth.

The largest use of gaming as a public relations and recruitment tool was the 2002 project *America's Army*, designed and released by the U.S. Army.

Marine Doom

In 1996, the United States Marine Corps adapted the popular shooting game *Doom 2* — in which a commando kills demons on Mars — into a training game called *Marine Doom*.

Played by multiple players over a local network, the game was intended to train marines to prepare for an attack, conserve ammunition, and follow the chain of command.

< This view of the terrain in *Marine Doom* features trenches, bunkers and barbed wire obstacles. The game was not a particularly realistic simulation of combat.

Canadian Armed Forces Virtual Reality

The Canadian Armed Forces began to experiment with virtual reality as a recruitment tool in 2015, after recruiters noticed they were competing directly with video game presentations at public events.

A civilian tries out the Canadian Armed Forces virtual reality firing range at a public event, 2020.

Computer Assisted Rehabilitation Environment (CAREN)

In 2011, the Canadian Armed Forces partnered with the Ottawa Hospital to launch the Rehabilitation Virtual Reality Lab.

The CAREN system pairs an immersive projection screen with a dual-belt treadmill. Some of its first users were Canadian soldiers who were fitted with prosthetic limbs after suffering amputations due to injuries incurred in Afghanistan.

Corporal Dale Cross conducts movement testing on a virtual simulator at the Ottawa Hospital, 2012.

CHAPTER 5

GAMING GLOBAL INSECURITY: 2014 TO THE PRESENT

Present-day game scenarios address complex problems: the shifting balance between world powers, climate change, and unforeseen events such as pandemics.

Since 2015, defence professionals have increasingly turned to war games to analyze and play through future scenarios and potential solutions. By recreating past and imaginary wars, games also allow the public to play for entertainment and to better understand modern conflicts.

Resource markers
from the *Aftershock*
humanitarian
rescue war game

Civil defence workers
help a woman get
through flood waters
in Azua, Dominican
Republic, following
Hurricane Laura,
August 23, 2020.

Operation LASER

The COVID-19 pandemic presented Canada with an unforeseen and rapidly unfolding crisis.

In 2020, the Canadian military was mobilized under Operation LASER to help mitigate the spread of the virus. Wargaming was one of the tools used by senior leadership to plan and prepare for this new mission.

Senior Canadian military staff are briefed on the plans for Operation LASER, April 2020.

Soldiers, civil servants, and police officers play *Aftershock* at a course on the protection of civilians at the Centro Conjunto para Operaciones de Paz de Chile (Chilean Joint Peacekeeping Operations Centre), April 2015.

PLANNING RESPONSES

Natural disasters, pandemics, and unconventional wars require imaginative solutions. Specialized games simulate present and future conflicts, help define problems, and suggest ways to coordinate responses.

In anticipating future threats and wars, militaries plan for, and game through, scenarios they hope will never take place.

Aftershock

This Canadian-designed game explores a hypothetical earthquake in a fictional country. The game tests the ability of different military, civilian, governmental and non-governmental actors to share resources, coordinate foreign aid, avoid epidemics, and provide humanitarian relief.

Players often fail unexpectedly due to unpredictable events in the game, providing a similar experience to the disorienting and chaotic aftermath of a real disaster.

The game boards for *Aftershock* show different districts of Gilasi, a fictional country, and where needs are most dire.

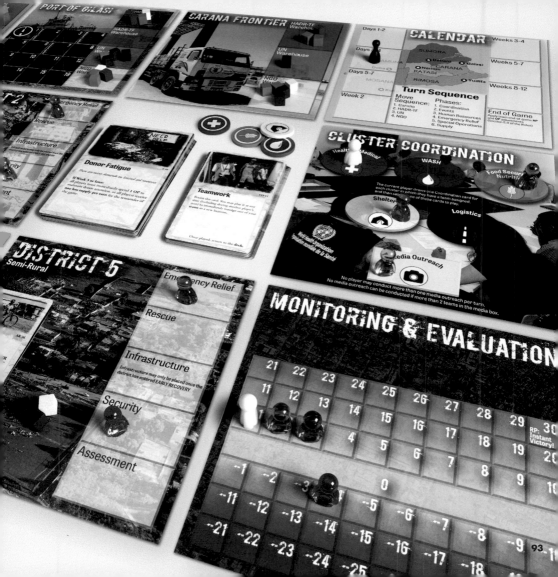

PORT OF GILASI

CARANA FRONTIER HADR-TF Warehouse

UN Warehouse

NGO

CALENDAR

Days 1-2   Weeks 3-4

Days   SUMORA

Days 5-7   Weeks 5-7

Week 2   Weeks 8-12

Turn Sequence

Move Sequence:
1. Carana
2. HADR-TF
3. UN
4. NGO

Phases:
1. Coordination
2. Events
3. Human Resources
4. Emergency Relief
5. Special Operations
6. Supply

End of Game
Apply team end-of-game RP and OP adjustments (Section 6.0 of the Rules)

Emergency Relief

Rescue

Infrastructure

Donor Fatigue

If Week 3 or later: all players must immediately spend 1 OP to maintain donor attention, or all players receive less supply per turn for the remainder of the game.

Teamwork

Retain this card. You may play it at any time (including during another player's turn) to immediately reassign one of your teams to a new location.

Once played, return to the deck.

CLUSTER-COORDINATION

Health & Medical   WASH   Food Security & Nutrition

Shelter   Logistics

World Health Organization
Organisation mondiale de la Santé

Media Outreach

The current player draws one Coordination card for each cluster in which they have a team assigned, and then selects one of those cards to play.

No player may conduct more than one media outreach per turn.
No media outreach can be conducted if more than 2 teams in the media box.

DISTRICT 5
Semi-Rural

Emergency Relief

Rescue

Infrastructure

Infrastructure may only be placed once the district has entered EARLY RECOVERY

Security

Assessment

MONITORING & EVALUATION

21	22	23	24	25	26	27	28	29	30
11	12	13	14	15	16	17	18	19	20
1	2	3	4	5	6	7	8	9	10
-1	-2	-3	0	-5	-6	-7	-8	-9	
-11	-12	-13	-14	-15	-16	-17	-18	-19	
-21	-22	-23	-24	-25		-16	-17	-18	

RP: 30 Instant Victory!

Young women playing *Tangling with Tigers* deliberate over their next move, advised by wargaming experts.

Tangling with Tigers

Girl Security, a U.S. organization founded to encourage young women to enter careers in national security, partnered with RAND Corporation wargaming specialists to develop this game.

Set on the Korean Peninsula, the game asks players to respond to a North Korean invasion of South Korea. With everything from conventional warfare to nuclear strikes on the table, players must make the "least worst" choices to defeat the invasion.

DR. YUNA WONG

Defence analyst at the Institute for Defense Analyses, Alexandria, Virginia

PERSPECTIVE

Yuna shares her insights as a professional wargamer:

"The games that the Pentagon commissions are classified and never see the light of day. The reason for releasing a commercial version of [one of the games I worked on] was to help the professional wargaming community . . . People could at least see at this moment in time what a strategic-level game that was used professionally looked like."

No shots are fired in *11-11: Memories Retold*. Players solve puzzles and follow the stories of a Canadian soldier and a German soldier on the Western Front.

MAKING MEANING THROUGH GAMES

Some people play games to remember past wars. Others do so to experience history in a safe and entertaining way.

Many contemporary game designers have abandoned conflict as a central gameplay mechanism. Instead, players are encouraged to work together to solve problems or build things.

Ross Rifles

Ross Rifles is a role-playing game in the tradition of *Dungeons and Dragons*, but about the First World War.

The game is named after the Canadian-made First World War rifle. Its goal is to help players better understand the challenges of trench warfare and the actions soldiers took to stay alive.

Players explore the experiences of Canadian soldiers in the First World War by choosing one of six roles: the Sergeant, the Recruit, the Artist, the Scrounger, the Scout, or the Scarred. Based on the play book for their role, players develop their soldier character as they play.

Illustration from *Ross Rifles* depicting "Provide Comfort," one of the actions a player can take to boost another player's morale in the game

Refugee Experiences

The mobile game *Bury Me, My Love* presents the fictional journey of Nour — a doctor escaping Syria's civil war — through text messages between her and her husband, Majd, who remains behind in Homs, Syria.

The game's writers based the story on news reporting about refugees and accounts by a Syrian woman who found refuge in France.

In the game *Bury Me, My Love*, Nour sends her husband a photo of her safe arrival in the European Union. >

GAME OVER – PLAY AGAIN?

War is a terrible human activity. So why do so many people enjoy games about war?

For some, it is a way to experience the past and to live vicariously through complex stories of historical conflicts. For others, the setting does not matter as much as the thrill of competing against other people or testing oneself.

War is not a game, yet militaries use games to learn, plan and train without the consequences of war.

And around the world, people of all ages and abilities continue to explore and learn about conflict through war games.

What will you play next?

Students play an educational war game at Georgetown University, 2022.

A COLLECTOR'S PERSPECTIVE

By David Stewart-Patterson

Could I win the Battle of Waterloo as Napoleon, conquer France as Kaiser Wilhelm, or capture Egypt as Rommel? Changing history was what lured me to war games.

I have played hundreds of games simulating historical wars and battles — simple and complex, short and long, tactical and strategic. I have played games using dice, cards, wooden blocks, cardboard counters, and miniature models.

JEU DU SIÉGE DE SÉBASTOPOL. 6.

A war game seems to be a contradiction in terms. War is about death and destruction. Games are about fellowship and fun. And yet, for centuries, people from all walks of life have enthusiastically played games about war.

Over the years, my interest has broadened from modern games about past wars to older games designed to reflect the wars of their times. I began collecting historical games published in times of war and peace, which themselves told stories about past conflicts.

In the 1800s, the "game of siege" was a popular type of war game. This French version, *Jeu du siège de Sébastopol*, reflected the battles, uniforms and equipment of the Crimean War (1853–1856).

One such game, the oldest in my collection — *Le Jeu des fortifications*, published in 1663 — was designed to teach students at France's Ecolle (sic) Royale Militaire about Sebastien Le Prestre de Vauban's innovative fortifications.

The game's designer, Gilles Jodelet, a fellow Royal Engineer, saw no conflict between having fun and preparing for the harsh business of war.

The publisher's dedication reads:

"I am not afraid of distracting you from any of your regular exercises by offering for your amusement a game that contains the basic principles of the art of war . . . Literature is studied at the academy of Louis the Great's famous school only insofar as it relates to places to attack and defend, assaults to launch and support, battles to win, and victories to achieve."

Historical war games deal with a wide array of subjects, such as industrial production and remembrance of war's triumphs and tragedies.

They also serve many purposes, including military recruitment and training, and boosting civilian morale. I am pleased to share games from my collection with the Canadian War Museum to help the Museum explore these and other themes in the **War Games** exhibition. You can see a few of my favourites on display, in this catalogue, and on my website, *gamesofwar.org*.

CONTRIBUTIONS

The **War Games** exhibition would not have been possible without the contribution of Haley Sharpe Design and the essential guidance of many of our colleagues at the Canadian War Museum and the Canadian Museum of History. We would like to thank, in particular: Maggie Arbour, Mona Ardestani, Britt Braaten, Jocelyn Brock, Claire Champ, Tim Cook, Jean Couture, Dave Deevey, Caroline Dromaguet, Ken Easton, Jenny Ellison, Eric Fernberg, Patricia Grimshaw, Brigitte Hamon, Shannyn Johnson, Vincent Lafond, Shirley Lam, Kathryn Lyons, Anne Macdonnell, Meredith Maclean, Peter MacLeod, Michael Miller, Mélanie Morin-Pelletier, Glenn Ogden, Dean Oliver, Sandra O'Quinn, Jem Pellerin, Katie Pollock, Jennifer Potter, Kirby Sayant, Alain Simard, James Whitham, Gabriel Yanicki, and Jimmy Youssef.

Finally, we would like to thank Steven Darby and Susan Ross for their outstanding photography, as well as Shannon Moore, Pascal Scallon-Chouinard, and Robyn Jeffrey for the production of this catalogue.

PHOTO CREDITS

Inside Cover   © Imperial War Museum (A 27819)

p. 9   (left) *Introduction of the Game of Chess at the Court of Anushirvan* (r 531–579) (reproduction), *Shahnamah* (Book of Kings) by Firdawsi, 16th century. Courtesy of the British Library.

p. 9   (right) Photo: Steven Darby, IMG2022-0180-0009-Dm | Artifact: Canadian Museum of History 89-574.2

p. 10   With permission of the Royal Ontario Museum, Toronto, Canada. © ROM.

p. 11   Courtesy of David Stewart-Patterson.

p. 12–13   Courtesy of the Canadian Go Association.

p. 14   With permission of the Royal Ontario Museum, Toronto, Canada. © ROM.

p. 17   Photo: IMG2022-0180-0006-Dm | Artifact: Canadian Museum of History 2021.17

p. 18   Courtesy of Angel Doxtater.

p. 20–21   Canadian War Museum 19830424-008

p. 21   Lieut. C.E. Nye / Canada. Dept. of National Defence / Library and Archives Canada / PA-108175

p. 22–23   *Illustrated London News*, March 6, 1909

p. 24   National Army Museum, United Kingdom, 1967-09-51

p. 26   Courtesy of Dominic Wells.

p. 26–27   *Illustrated London Times*, 1913

p. 28–29   Courtesy of David Stewart-Patterson.

p. 30–31   *HMCS Ville de Québec Gets a Sub*, painted by Harold Beament in 1943. Beaverbrook Collection of War Art, Canadian War Museum 19710261-1031

p. 32–33   © Imperial War Museum (A27822)

p. 34   © Imperial War Museum (A27819)

p. 35   Courtesy of the Western Approaches Headquarters Museum, Liverpool, UK.

p. 36   Canadian War Museum 20130161-029

p. 37   Courtesy of David Stewart-Patterson.

p. 38   Courtesy of David Stewart-Patterson.

p. 40–41   Canadian War Museum 20060124-001_b

p. 43   (left) Courtesy of the *Toronto Telegram*, Clara Thomas Archives and Special Collections, York University.

p. 43   (right) Canadian War Museum 1981032-010_a

p. 44–45   Photo: Steven Darby, IMG2022-0180-007-Dm | Artifacts: Canadian Museum of History 2009.71.1394.1 a-b

p. 46   Courtesy of David Stewart-Patterson.

p. 47   Courtesy of The Strong National Museum of Play, Rochester, New York.

p. 48–49   Photo: IMG2022-0180-0012-Dm-2 | Artifacts: Canadian Museum of History 2009.71.1082.1 a-b

p. 49   Courtesy of Daniel Kwan.

p. 50   Courtesy of Ammar Ijaz.